X

<u>Shifting Shifting</u>

Published by / Herausgegeben vom Camden Arts Centre, London
in collaboration with / in Zusammenarbeit mit The Fruitmarket Gallery,
Edinburgh, Bergen Kunsthall and Kunstverein Hannover.

Contents / Inhalt

Foreword

There is a strong physical appeal to Aernout Mik's work; it draws you in and includes you so that you become part of the event and complicit with the action. The sculptural relationship of wall to floor and the spatial play between a built environment and a filmed one are intrinsic to how Mik's videos are experienced.

Shifting Shifting comprises four works made in the past eighteen months; *Vacuum Room* (2005), *Scapegoats* (2006), *Raw Footage* (2006) and *Training Ground* (2006). Puzzling, bizarre but intensely familiar, these films have at their heart an insight into the exercise and shifting distribution of power, the repeated patterns of human behaviour and the disquieting ordinariness of extraordinary situations.

With the exception of *Raw Footage* these works are constructed fictions with no clear beginning and with little sense of where anything might end. And, as always with Mik's work, there is no classic cinematic narrative or sound. The actions played out in a heightened sense of realism and with an almost absurd attention to detail, chime unnervingly with many shared anxieties of recent times – but this being Aernout Mik, it is done with a lightness of touch and a deft sense of humour.

Raw Footage, however, is created from unused documentary footage taken during the war in former Yugoslavia. Now over a decade old, this material was never broadcast at the time because of its lack of dramatic content.

Using 'found' footage for the first ever time, Mik reveals the banality of war which television news typically edits out and at the same time reminds us that certain truths are just as strange as fiction. With this work, unlike the others, the images are not screened at floor level with the result that, as with television, the viewer's relationship is more cerebral than physical.

The anthropologist Michael Taussig was invited by Mik to write an essay for this catalogue. His absorbing text expands vividly on those moments of recognition, when the knowledge of Mik's invented world frames the reality of human behaviour and lived experience.

We are extremely grateful to Michael Taussig for his wholehearted involvement with the project and to Irma Boom, who has worked closely with Aernout Mik to produce a book which is beautifully designed and in harmony with his work.

Shifting Shifting has been organised collaboratively by four institutions, from four different European countries. All of us are united by a long standing and deeply felt interest in the work of Aernout Mik. The exhibition and publication have been carefully co-ordinated by Bruce Haines, Exhibitions Organiser at Camden Arts Centre, and has been made possible by a generous grant to be shared across the organisations from the Mondriaan Foundation towards the exhibition tour; and the Royal Netherlands Embassy in London. Both these organisations are noted for their adventurous funding policies and continued support for Dutch artists and the institutions that show them. We also extend our thanks to Ulrich Gebauer and Andreas Bunte from carlier | gebauer, Berlin who represent Mik's work and who have helped enormously with the realisation of the exhibition.

It has been a very great pleasure for all of us to work with Aernout Mik; we have enjoyed his intelligence, insight and wit, appreciating above all his hard work and commitment to showing these four remarkable video installations in London, Edinburgh, Bergen and Hannover.

Jenni Lomax, Director, Camden Arts Centre, London

On behalf of
Dr. Fiona Bradley, Director, The Fruitmarket Gallery, Edinburgh
Solveig Øvstebø, Director, Bergen Kunsthall
Dr. Stephan Berg, Director, Kunstverein Hannover

Flying over the Atlantic to Europe while watching AM's videos on my Apple computer, the man next to me had some sort of attack, provoking a scene not unlike those I was viewing on my computer screen. I take this to be pure coincidence, yet nevertheless suggestive of the strange power in AM's artworks which irresistibly call out to me as *aeronautical* on account of the gyrations they produce as to what is real and what is staged and why it seems to matter so much that you must get it right before the plane lands or the corpses turn out to be real and not actors acting, or is it the other way around? The man could barely breathe yet seemed calm, maybe too calm. He was seated three empty seats to my side and at first I noted nothing untoward. I was wearing earphones, my hearing was muffled, and it was dark, the plane boring through the night sky.

"Boring through the night sky". This sounds exciting, mythical, and romantic, but you know how it is in planes these days and has been for a long time. None of those things. People don't even look out the windows any more. Indeed, they are instructed to pull down the shades so as to better see the airline videos whose task it is to provide excitement, myth, and romance, possibly involving aeroplanes boring through the night. The amazing fact is that we are over thirty thousand feet high in the air, separated from the cold ethereality of the endless sky and the planet below by a thin membrane of aluminum. Yet this means absolutely nothing.

This, in a nutshell, is what AM's artwork makes me think about: the routinisation of the fantastic, and the strangeness of the familiar.

Things have changed over the past few years. So much of reality and what we call 'world events' comes through TV and video that we have,

without knowing it, become different creatures because of our new eye.
But AM's artwork turns this very same eye in on itself. It makes you aware of this new eye of ours; you feel how thin the membrane is between you and the earth, thousands of feet below.

However, the way you become aware of this is not straightforward. Nor could it be given the traps and deceptions involved. There is no straightforward way of understanding how you understand. To see this new eye of yours means, first off, the recognition that you are seeing it with that very same eye. To get around this impasse requires something like visual-psychotherapy in which you have to battle with the puzzle of the paradox and deal with the contradiction, the false leads and the ambiguity, such that the surest course is a zigzag.

For example, AM's videos exude calm, like the man seeming to die three seats from me as we bored through the night with just stars for company. Yet as with that man, it is a perturbing calm.

When AM has an entire video showing people jumping up and down in a park, their fantastic behaviour is rendered banal by repetition and the look on their faces. Banality here is not really calm but a calm that disturbs, *a calm out of place*. How can that be?

The same applies to the crazy behaviour of the rebels, as much as the infuriated administrators and politicians they confront, in *Vacuum Room*. Again and again we find this, as with the video of people and sheep milling around an overturned bus by the highway, or with the police training exercise . . .

Aernout Mik
Park, 2002

Aernout Mik
Refraction, 2004

I believe Hannah Arendt called this sort of thing the "banality of evil" and was much criticized for this idea as she applied it to Eichmann as the all too typical non-aggressive aggressor, the all too typical cog in the genocide machine. The Israeli government wanted his trial in Jerusalem to be a show trial and portray Eichmann as a monster – a captured monster – at the centre of the show. But Arendt went deeper. Her great insight was to demonstrate how it was the ordinariness of his persona that was monstrous.[1]

When AM shows skinny, unkempt boy soldiers of about fourteen years of age deftly pricking grown men and women in the back with the point of their machine guns in the video called *Scapegoats,* the meandering, mind-numbing banality rises even more to the surface of what should be – you would think – the heart-renderingly spectacular events of war and cruelty. Yet is it not the case, as evidenced here, that this calm makes it ever so much more creepy? In this video, grown men and women sometimes lurch forward and beat up on an elderly man crouching over to protect himself. Antagonists and victims alike seem more like wound up rubbery dolls than humans, yet – and this is surely the point – they are, because of that appearance, all the more human. You yourself could be that kid fondling his toy which is a gun. You yourself could be that woman or man in a raggedy-tag uniform, suddenly for no obvious reason, attacking the old man. There they go, smoking too many cigarettes (lifelines to God), wandering round and round the large holding pens, football stadiums or gyms, lining up the prisoners, suddenly exploding in paroxysms of anger for no obvious reason.

Aernout Mik
Scapegoats, 2006

The motion of the soldiers and prisoners in this sports stadium is itself worth a few words for I am reminded of grazing sheep or cattle. The soldiers sometimes seem to have a plan and yet at other times seem to act randomly. Strangely, this applies almost as much to the prisoners as well. And at times there is a blurring of the two 'sides' so you can't tell who is who. There is a constant impulse to move and for movement, like a nervous tic that is, I think, disturbing to the viewer. What is more, the movement is unpredictable, consisting of sudden accelerations followed by zones of calm and smoothness, like animals grazing in a field, happy in their munching. Look at the elderly man in *Scapegoats* attending to his cooking in a makeshift kitchen, oblivious to the holocaust cooking all around him. Chicken stew. Yum, yum. It all seems so utterly normal. Utterly, utterly normal, boring normal, like watching the human ribcage expand and deflate in its monotonous, natural necessity.

A lot of this depends on using an 'ethnographic eye' so as to get around what I call our *new eye*, the one created by the TV/video complex for reportage of world events and crises. The ethnographic eye I have in mind focuses on the small, everyday, realities that make up life without us ever quite realising their existence. The ethnographic eye frames, exposes and alienates the habitual, so deeply ingrained you never saw it. It is a little like listening to your own heartbeat magnified by an echocardiogram. You are suddenly made aware of the grain of existence, of what we call the obvious – only it was so obvious that you have remained unaware. It only becomes obvious once it has been pointed out.

This is similar to Walter Benjamin's claims for film as supplying an "optical unconscious", bringing out properties of phenomena we didn't dream existed. Photography can bring out "the physiognomic aspects of visual worlds which dwell in the smallest things", he wrote, "meaningful yet covert enough to find a hiding place in waking dreams, but which, enlarged yet capable of formulations, make the difference between technology and magic visible as a thoroughly historical variable".[2]

Yet AM's videos make you ponder "which is magical and which is not?" Is not TV news magical precisely because of its technological appearance? Are not AM's videos magical because they are so aimless and matter of fact? This confusion comes about, I think, because there is still hope, as when Benjamin writes of the "hiding place in waking dreams". It is this place that AM's videos lead us to and excavate. He uses magic to dislodge magic, an apotropaic art.

By letting the camera play back and forth for no apparent reason – this is a motiveless camera – the activities filmed seem weird. In one sense the activities are ordinary, super-ordinary. But by being filmed this way they become alienated. This is another one of those 'tricks' used by AM so as to makes us aware of our new third eye, using it, so to speak, so as to get a good hard look at itself. By focusing on the sludge of the everyday in its smallest details and allowing repetition and boredom to have their play, the viewer has room to speculate and wander in and out of the tunnel of narrative.

Sure it is that the absence of sound contributes to the sense of banality which I define as *calm out of place*. The silence can seem like an invitation to think, to reinterpret what you are seeing. The silence makes for a question. The silence makes for mystery. "What the hell is going on here? Why is there no sound? God! Now I have to think for myself!" The silence makes what you see seem incomplete. You feel a mystery. You have been shut out of something. Where is the beginning? Where are we going? You feel a mystery. So you look harder.

Not only is there an absence of sound but there is an absence of story. There is no voice spinning a narrative. What makes the soundlessness so especially significant, however, is the implicit but overpowering contrast with Fox and CNN news where the sound, especially the story told by a human or supposedly human voice, is fundamental. Not to have it is to be cast adrift. "Now I have to work it out myself."

I look up from my AM video and watch the man three seats from me. A stewardess with short blonde hair and a wonderfully kind smile has arrived and with the help of a young steward is arranging a bottle of oxygen by the man's side so he can breath through a mask. The little scene is illuminated by a narrow cone of light from the overhead lamp. The rest of the cabin is dark and the rest of the passengers on this fairly empty flight seem asleep. The stewardess is crouching in the aisle so her face is level with the sick man's face. She is reassuring him while at the same time she is astutely studying his face and behaviour and getting his medical history. In fact, it is through this study and those questions that she is being so reassuring. The man relaxes. She is normalising the crisis and this is surely a good thing to do in this situation. What could be more frightening than a heart attack mid-air? Later on I learn she actually is

a professional nurse as well as an airline stewardess. The combination of skills here is symbiotic. As stewardess and nurse she is caretaker supreme, one whose leading characteristics are the normalisation of crisis, while at the back of her mind, hidden from view, is that galloping panic that *Yes!* This is a very shitty situation.

While she pours calm on troubled waters, the calm out of place displayed in AM's videos are the trouble.

She and her patient are acting out a real life drama. They have moved reality into another plane of reality, another theatre of the real that is both deadly real yet also an act. It is this entanglement that AM's artwork engages.

Normalisation of the abnormal is what you will see again and again in AM's artwork, but with yet another trick involving our third eye and that is that the people in his videos are actors. With one exception (that I know of), he is not filming real events, and that exception is *Raw Footage* – made out of discarded fragments of film or video footage by commercial news organisations. I think therefore of *Raw Footage* as the base-line artwork of AM's corpus even though it is the latest or one of the latest.

Why is it base-line? Is it because it works with what was discarded as too meaningless or too ordinary? Is it because at the very same time it concerns ethnic cleansing in former Yugoslavia? Put the two together. It is a terrible thing. You think that nothing could be more passionate and Dionysian, crazed and exuberant, than ethnic cleansing. Yet here we are in dullsville, the sludge that allows the dailiness of organised hate to flourish.

They say you need a thief to catch a thief, and this is what AM's videos are doing with their pseudo-events mimicking real events so as to show their 'made-up-ness'. AM's videos imitate the dramas portrayed by our news organisations together with the visuality of our new, third eye; but AM's videos imitate with a difference. They overlap with the new eye, so that all the more powerfully, they draw apart.

This is what happens in two classic ethnographic films that have influenced AM, Jean Rouch's *Les Maîtres Fous*3 and Gerry Leach's *Trobriand Cricket*.4 In these films, the overlap is strikingly obvious, on account of the race and colonial difference between the mimics and what they are mimicking. When Jean Rouch's mid 1950s Niger emigrants to Ghana imitate French and British colonial officers, living or dead, you get a very doubled message. The mimicry is striking, yet so is the difference manifest between the mimics and the mimicked, whereas in AM's videos, this difference is erased. He is not filming in the colony but in the metropole, so you never feel secure as to what is real and what is being acted. The more clear you are that what you are watching is faked, the more you will marvel at how like true life such faking is, not because AM's videos mimic the dramatic forms of our news broadcasts and photographs, but precisely because they do not.

Mick Taussig, November 2006

Jean Rouch
Les Maîtres Fous, 1955

1 'Eichmann in Jerusalem: A Report on the Banality of Evil', Hannah Arendt, (1963). Arendt, a political theorist, fled Germany during Hitler's rise to power. This book was published after she reported on Adolf Eichmann's trial for The New Yorker and observed that Eichmann neither showed any trace of anti-Semitism nor psychological damage and that psychologists had remarked that Eichmann's attitude towards other people, especially his family and friends, was "highly desirable", while another remarked that the only unusual trait Eichmann displayed was being more "normal" in his habits and speech than the average person.

2 Walter Benjamin, 'A Small History of Photography,' *One-Way Street and Other Writings*, trans. E. Jephcott and K. Shorter (London: New Left Books, 1979), pp 243-44

3 *Les Maîtres Fous*, (Mad Masters), directed by Jean Rouch (1954, 35 mins). Jean Rouch filmed the annual ceremony of an African religious sect, the Hauka, in which they entered a trance and were possessed by various spirits associated with Western colonial powers: the governor-general, the engineer, the doctor's wife, the wicked major and the corporal of the guard. The film shows men with rolling eyes, foaming at the mouth, eating a sacrificed dog and burning their bodies with torches. Rouch's film was a key influence behind Werner Herzog's film *Heart of Glass* (1975) in which Herzog hypnotized the cast to give their acting, and so the whole film, a more dreamlike quality.

4   *Trobriand Cricket: An Ingenious Response to Colonialism*, directed by Jerry W. Leach, (1975, 53 mins). *Trobriand Cricket* is a famous ethnographic film documenting the way the game of cricket has come to take on a different form and significance since it was introduced by Methodist missionaries into the Trobriand islands in the early 20th century. The islanders' mimicry of this traditional colonial game is not a slavish copy but instead creates new forms and parody as well, such that it is the sort of anthropology which makes the Westerner aware of his or her cultural preconceptions.

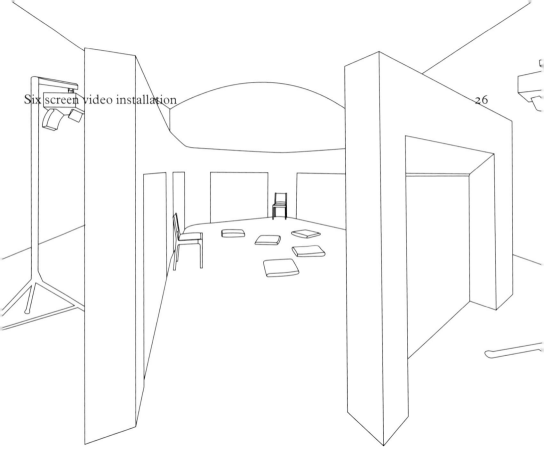

Six screen video installation

26

<u>Vacuum Room</u>
2005

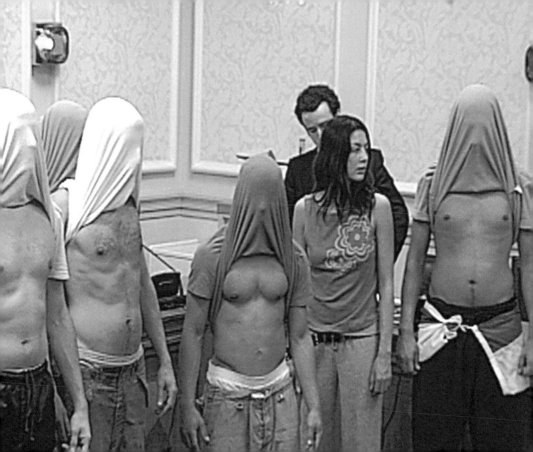

.

.

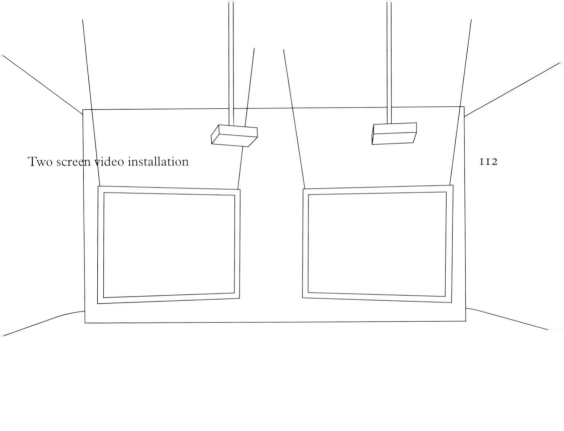

Two screen video installation

112

<u>Raw Footage</u>
2006

.

Raw Footage   136

Raw Footage

.

.

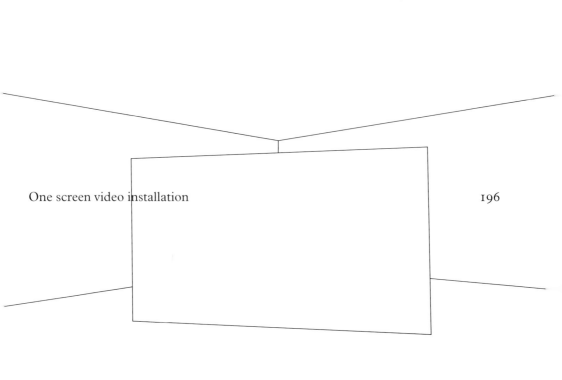

One screen video installation   196

<u>Scapegoats</u>
2006

Scapegoats

Scapegoats   230

Scapegoats

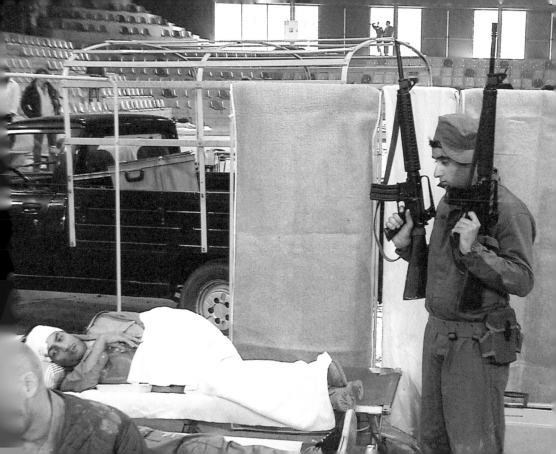

.

Scapegoats

Scapegoats   262

.

Scapegoats 270

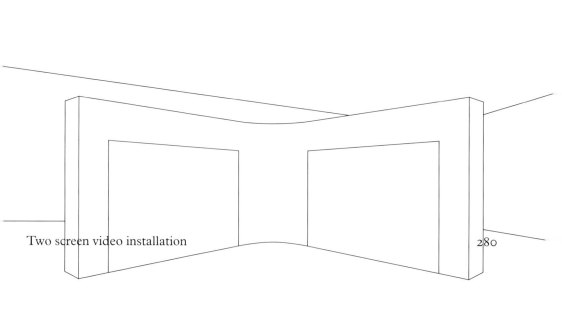

Two screen video installation

280

Training Ground

2006

Während ich über den Atlantik nach Europa flog und auf meinem Apple Computer Videos von AM anschaute, hatte der Mann in der Sitzreihe neben mir eine Art Anfall. Dabei beschwor er eine Szene herauf, die so ähnlich war wie diejenigen, die ich auf meinem Bildschirm sah. Ich glaube, das war der reine Zufall. Aber dennoch schien mir das charakteristisch zu sein für die seltsame Kraft der Kunst von AM, die ich in unwiderstehlicher Weise als aeronautisch empfinde wegen ihrer turbulenten Verwirrspiele. Man weiß nie, was wirklich und was inszeniert ist. Und warum es so wichtig wird, dass man das rauskriegt, noch bevor das Flugzeug landet und die Leichen sich plötzlich als echt erweisen und nicht als Schauspieler, die den Tod nur spielen. Oder ist es anders herum richtig? Der Mann neben mir konnte kaum noch atmen, aber er schien gefasst zu sein, vielleicht etwas zu gefasst. Er saß drei Plätze entfernt von mir, die leer geblieben waren, und zuerst war er mir gar nicht aufgefallen. Ich trug ein Ohrstöpsel-Mikrofon, mein Gehörsinn war gedämpft, und das Flugzeug flog durch einen dunklen Nachthimmel.

‚Durch den dunklen Nachthimmel fliegen.' Das klingt aufregend, mythisch und romantisch. Aber Sie wissen ja, wie das heute – und schon lange – mit dem Fliegen ist. So ist es nicht. Die Menschen schauen noch nicht einmal mehr aus dem Fenster. Tatsächlich bittet man sie, die Fenster zu verdunkeln, damit sie die Videos der Fluggesellschaft besser sehen können. Die sollen dann für eine aufregende, mythische und romantische Stimmung sorgen. Vielleicht auch für eine, in der Flugzeuge durch einen dunklen Nachthimmel fliegen. Was wirklich erstaunlich ist: Wir fliegen 30 000 Fuß hoch in der Luft und sind von der Kälte draußen und der Erde unter uns nur durch eine dünne Aluminiummembran getrennt. Und doch bedeutet das alles gar nichts.

Im Kern ist es das, worüber mich AMs Werke nachdenken lassen: über die Normalität des Fantastischen und über das Fantastische des Normalen.

Die Dinge haben sich in den letzten Jahren verändert. Ganz viel Wirklichkeit und was wir ,Weltereignisse' nennen, lernen wir durch Fernseh- und Videobilder kennen. Und ohne dass es uns bewusst wird, werden diese Bilder durch unser neues Auge zu neuen Wesenheiten. AMs Werke lenken dieses Auge auf sich selbst zurück. Sie sorgen dafür, dass wir uns unseres neuen Auges bewusst werden. Dann merken wir auch, wie dünn die Membran ist zwischen uns und der Erde, 30 000 Fuß unter uns.

Dieses Bewusstsein entwickelt sich indes nicht in direkter Weise. Und auch nicht ohne Fallen und Enttäuschungen. Es gibt keinen direkten Weg, um zu begreifen, wie man begreift. Um dieses neue Auge zu erkennen, gilt es, sich von der Vorstellung zu lösen, man würde es mit demselben Auge erkennen können. Diese Sackgasse zu vermeiden, erfordert so etwas wie eine visuelle Psychotherapie. In ihr schlägt man sich mit den Rätseln des Paradoxen herum und muss mit Widersprüchen fertig werden. Zweideutigkeit und Falschheit führen, und der sicherste Weg ist der Zickzackkurs.

Ein Beispiel. AMs Videos wirken ganz ruhig. So ruhig wie der Mann, der drei Sitze weg von mir gerade zu sterben scheint, während wir durch die Nacht fliegen, wobei uns nur die Sterne Gesellschaft leisten. Genau so irritierend wie die Ruhe des Mannes ist die Ruhe von AMs Videos.

Aernout Mik
Park, 2002

Aernout Mik
Refraction, 2004

Sehen wir in einem Video von AM, wie Menschen in einem Park herumhüpfen, wird ihr bizarres Verhalten durch die Wiederholung und den Ausdruck ihrer Gesichter zu etwa ganz Alltäglichem. Aber die Alltäglichkeit erscheint nicht wirklich normal. Die Normalität wirkt verstörend. Als unangemessene Ruhe. Wie ist das möglich?

Dasselbe gilt für das verrückte Verhalten der Rebellen wie für die wütenden Beamten und Politiker, gegen die sie im *Vacuum Room* antreten. Wir begegnen dem immer wieder, im Video mit den Menschen und Schafen, die ziellos um den umgekippten Bus auf dem Highway herumlaufen, oder in dem Video mit dem Trainingslager der Polizei ...

Ich glaube, Hannah Arendt hat das die „Banalität des Bösen" genannt. Sie wurde sehr dafür kritisiert, als sie diesen Begriff auf Eichmann anwandte als dem Prototyp des unaggressiven Aggressors, das typische Rädchen in der Maschinerie des Völkermords. Die israelische Regierung wollte diesen Prozess damals als Musterprozess führen, in dem Eichmann als Ungeheuer – als gefangenes Ungeheuer – figurieren sollte. Aber Arendt lotete tiefer. Ihrem Verständnis verdanken wir die Einsicht, wie monströs die Normalität eines Menschen sein kann.[1]

Zeigt AM in dem Video *Scapegoats* dünne, ungekämmte Kindersoldaten, die mit ihren vielleicht vierzehn Jahren erwachsenen Männern und Frauen heftig die Mündungen ihrer Maschinengewehre in die Rücken stoßen, dann wird dem Betrachter deutlich, wie absolut alltäglich hier eine irrationale und abstumpfende Praxis geworden ist, von der man glauben sollte, sie gehöre allein in die Ausnahmesituation eines Herz zerreißenden, grausamen Krieges. Aber macht die ruhige Selbstverständlichkeit, mit der sich die Dinge hier nachweislich vollziehen, diese nicht noch schauriger? Im selben Video treten ab und zu erwachsene Männer und Frauen vor, um einen älteren Mann zu schlagen, der sich zusammenkrümmt, um sich so besser zu schützen. Das Verhalten von Tätern und Opfern wirkt eher wie das von aufgezogenen Puppen als von Menschen. Und doch – und das ist mit Sicherheit die Pointe – wirken sie darum nur umso menschlicher. Jeder von uns könnte eines dieser Kinder sein, die mit ihrem Gewehr herumfuchteln wie mit einem Spielzeug. Jeder von uns könnte einer dieser Männer oder Frauen in einer abgerissenen Uniform sein, die plötzlich ohne erkennbaren Grund den alten Mann angreifen. Da gehen sie und rauchen zu viele Zigaretten (ihre Lebenslinien zu Gott), sie halten Füller in der Hand, wandern auf und ab, lassen ihre Gefangenen in Fußballstadien oder Arenen aufmarschieren, und plötzlich explodieren sie in Zorn und Gewalt ohne erkennbaren Grund.

Allein die Bewegung der Soldaten und Gefangenen in diesem Sportstadium ist eine Betrachtung wert, denn sie erinnert mich an die von grasendem Vieh oder von Schafen. Manchmal scheinen die Soldaten dabei einem Vorsatz zu folgen, dann wieder sieht alles aus wie ganz zufällig. Merkwürdigerweise trifft das genauso für die Bewegung der Gefangenen zu. Und manchmal verschwimmen die beiden ‚Seiten‘ ineinander, so dass man nicht mehr sagen kann, wer da wer ist. Es gibt ein ständiges Bedürfnis nach Bewegung. Das ist wie ein nervöser Tick und für den Betrachter höchst verwirrend. Darüber hinaus ist diese Bewegung völlig unvorhersehbar. Manchmal gehen die Menschen sehr schnell, dann wieder ruhig und langsam wie Tiere, die auf einer Wiese grasen und zufrieden vor sich hinkäuen. Schauen wir uns den älteren Mann in *Scapegoats* an, wie er sich in seiner provisorischen Küche auf das Kochen konzentriert! Er vergisst dabei vollkommen den Holocaust. Er kocht nur noch. Ein Hühnchenragout. Lecker. Alles scheint so normal zu sein. Total normal. Auf öde Weise normal. Als beobachte man, wie der Brustkorb eines Menschen sich beim Atmen erweitert und wieder zusammenzieht. Monoton, natürlich, notwendig.

Viel hängt davon ab, dass man dabei das ‚Auge eines Ethnografen‘ benutzt, um so zum Blick unseres *neuen Auges* vorzustoßen, wie ich es genannt habe. Fernsehen und Video schufen es, um Weltereignisse und Krisen im großen Stil zu dokumentieren. Das ethnografische Auge, das mir vorschwebt, konzentriert sich auf die scheinbar unbedeutende, alltägliche Wirklichkeit, aus der sich das Leben zusammensetzt, ohne dass wir uns das überhaupt klar machen. Das ethnografische Auge rahmt, belichtet und stellt das Gewohnte und Gewöhnliche, das so tief in unserem Bewusstsein verankert ist, dass wir es nie wahrgenommen haben, als fremd aus. Es ist, als würden wir unserem eigenen Herzschlag lauschen, den ein Elektrokardiogramm hörbar gemacht hat. Plötzlich erkennen wir die Essenz unserer Existenz, was wir das Offenbare nennen. Nur war es so offenbar, dass wir es gar nicht mehr wahrgenommen haben. Offenbar wird es erst, nachdem es belichtet und herausgestellt wurde.

Ganz ähnlich, behauptet Walter Benjamin, bringt die Fotografie ein ‚Optisch-Unbewusstes‘ zum Ausdruck. Sie zeigt uns Eigenschaften der

Aernout Mik
Scapegoats, 2006

Dinge, von denen wir nicht einmal geträumt hätten, dass sie diese besitzen. „Zugleich eröffnet die Fotografie", so schrieb er, „in diesem Material die physiognomischen Aspekte, Bildwelten, welche im Kleinsten wohnen, deutbar und verborgen genug, um in Wachträumen Unterschlupf gefunden zu haben, nun aber, groß und formulierbar wie sie geworden sind, die Differenz zwischen Technik und Magie als durch und durch historische Variable sichtbar zu machen."[2]

AMs Videos lassen uns darüber nachsinnen, „was magisch ist und was nicht?" Sind Fernsehnachrichten nicht genau darum magisch, weil sie so technisch aussehen? Sind AMs Videos magisch, weil sie so ziellos und selbstverständlich daherkommen? Die Ursache der Verwirrung rührt, wie ich glaube, daher, dass es noch Hoffnung gibt, wie wenn Benjamin vom ‚Versteck in Wachträumen' schreibt. Dahin, zu dieser Ausgrabungsstätte, führen uns AMs Videos. Er nutzt Magie zur Aushebung von Magie. Eine apotropäische Kunst.

Indem er seine Kamera ohne ersichtlichen Grund vor- und zurückspulen lässt – es ist eine ziellos agierende Kamera – erscheinen die gefilmten Handlungen äußerst merkwürdig. Einerseits sind sie ganz alltäglich, außerordentlich alltäglich. Aber auf diese Weise gefilmt, erscheinen sie sehr fremdartig. Das ist wieder einer von AM Tricks. So macht er uns unser drittes Auge bewusst. Er benutzt es, damit es sich sozusagen direkt und genau selbst anblickt. Indem es sich auf das Banale und Alltägliche in allen Details konzentriert und dabei Wiederholung und Langeweile zulässt, hat der Betrachter Raum für Spekulationen und kann in die Erzählung hineinwandern und aus ihr heraus.

Mit Sicherheit trägt die Abwesenheit des Tones mit zum Eindruck einer Alltäglichkeit bei, die ich als *unangemessene Ruhe* bezeichne. Diese Ruhe kann wie eine Einladung zum Denken wirken. Eine Einladung, was man sieht, neu zu deuten. Das Schweigen fordert zur Frage auf. Das Schweigen bildet ein Rätsel. ‚Was zum Teufel geht hier vor? Warum gibt es keinen Ton? Gott, jetzt muss ich selbst nachdenken!' Das Schweigen lässt das Gesehene unvollständig erscheinen. Wir fühlen ein Geheimnis. Wir fühlen uns ausgeschlossen. Wo ist der Anfang? Wohin gehen wir? Wir fühlen ein Geheimnis. Wir schauen genauer hin.

Es gibt nicht nur die Abwesenheit des Tones, sondern auch die Abwesenheit einer Erzählung. Keine Stimme erzählt uns eine Geschichte. Was das Schweigen jedoch so bedeutungsvoll macht, ist der implizit gegebene Gegensatz zu den Nachrichten von Fox und CNN, bei denen die Tonspur, vor allem die kommentierende menschliche Stimme, fundamental ist. Wenn sie nicht mehr da ist, wird der Betrachter aus der Bahn geworfen. ‚Jetzt muss ich mir selbst einen Reim auf alles machen.'

Ich schaue von AMs Video hoch und auf den Mann drei Sitze entfernt von mir. Eine Stewardess mit kurzem, blondem Haar und einem wunderbar warmen Lächeln ist gerade zu ihm gekommen und richtet, unterstützt von einem jungen Steward, eine Sauerstoffflasche bei ihm ein, damit der Mann durch eine Maske atmen kann. Die kleine Szene wird durch den schmalen Lichtkegel der Leselampe über dem Sitz beleuchtet. Ansonsten ist die Kabine dunkel, und die übrigen Passagiere dieses nur schwach gebuchten Fluges scheinen zu schlafen. Die Stewardess arbeitet sich zum Sitz des kranken Mannes vor. Ihr Gesicht ist jetzt auf Höhe seines Gesichtes. Sie redet ihm in beruhigender Weise zu, während sie gleichzeitig ganz genau sein Gesicht und sein Verhalten studiert, um herauszubekommen, was ihm fehlt. Genau dieses Verhalten zusammen mit ihren Fragen lässt sie so beruhigend wirken. Der Mann entspannt sich. Sie normalisiert die Krise, und das ist wahrscheinlich das Beste, was sie in dieser Situation tun kann. Was könnte schrecklicher sein als ein Herzanfall hier oben während des Flugs? Später erfahre ich, dass sie nicht nur Stewardess, sondern auch ausgebildete Krankenschwester ist. Die Verbindung ihrer Fähigkeiten stellt eine schöne Symbiose dar. Als Stewardess und Krankenschwester ist sie die Fürsorge in Person. Jemand, der dafür gemacht ist, Krisen zu normalisieren, während sie in ihrem Kopf, ohne dass es sichtbar würde, eine aufkommende Panik zurückdrängt, die Einsicht: Ja, das ist eine ziemlich beschissene Situation.

Während sie eine Besorgnis erregende Situation beruhigt, ist die unangemessene Ruhe in AMs Videos das Besorgnis Erregende.

Sie und ihr Patient agieren ein Drama im wirklichen Leben aus. Sie verschieben dabei die Wirklichkeit auf eine andere Wirklichkeitsebene. In ein Theater des Wirklichen, das zugleich tödlich real wie auch ein theatralischer Akt ist. Diese Verknüpfung findet sich auch in AMs Werken.

Die Normalisierung des Anormalen sieht man immer wieder in AMs Werken. Dabei hält er noch einen weiteren Trick parat, der unser drittes Auge einbezieht. Es handelt sich darum, dass die Menschen seiner Videos Schauspieler sind. Mit einer einzigen Ausnahme (von der ich weiß) hat er keine wirklichen Ereignisse gefilmt. Diese Ausnahme ist *Raw Footage*. Sie besteht aus ausgesonderten Film- und Videoschnipseln kommerzieller

Nachrichtensender. Daher halte ich *Raw Footage* für das grundlegende Kunstwerk im Œuvre von AM überhaupt, obwohl es seine aktuellste oder doch eine der aktuelleren Arbeiten ist.

Warum ist sie grundlegend? Weil sie mit ausgemustertem Material arbeitet, das als zu bedeutungslos oder zu gewöhnlich ausgesondert wurde? Weil es in ihr darüber hinaus um ethnische Säuberung im ehemaligen Jugoslawien geht? Nehmen wir beides zusammen! Es ist schrecklich. Sie glauben, nichts könnte leidenschaftlicher und dionysischer, verrückter und überschäumender sein als eine ethnische Säuberung. Aber wir sind hier in einer gewöhnlichen Tretmühle, in einer schäbigen Routine, wo der organisierte Hass jeden Tag neu aufflammt.

Man sagt, es bräuchte einen Dieb, um einen Dieb zu fangen. Genau das machen AMs Videos, wenn ihre Pseudoereignisse reale Ereignisse imitieren, um so ihren Inszenierungscharakter auszustellen. AMs Videos stellen die Dramen nach, die unsere Nachrichtensender liefern, wobei unser neues drittes Auge mit im Spiel ist. Dabei imitieren AMs Videos mit einem Unterschied. Weil sie mit dem neuen Auge interferieren, fallen sie umso stärker auseinander.

Das geschieht auch in zwei Klassikern des ethnografischen Films, die AM beeinflusst haben, in Jean Rouchs *Les Maîtres Fous*[3] und in Gerry Leachs *Trobriand Cricket*.[4] In diesen Filmen hat die Interferenz ganz auffällig und offenkundig mit rassischen und kolonialen Unterschieden zwischen den Imitierenden und den Imitierten zu tun. Wenn in Jean Rouchs Film Mitte der fünfziger Jahre Emigranten aus Niger in Ghana französische und britische Kolonialoffiziere nachahmen, gleichgültig ob lebende oder tote, ist die Botschaft für den Betrachter doppeldeutig. Die Mimikry ist offenkundig, aber genauso offenkundig ist auch der Unterschied zwischen den Imitierenden und den Imitierten. Indes ist in AMs Videos dieser Unterschied ausgelöscht. Er filmt nicht in der Kolonie, sondern in der Hauptstadt. Dabei weiß der Betrachter nie so genau, was nun wirklich und was inszeniert ist. Umso genauer man weiß, dass man einer Mimikry zuschaut, umso mehr staunt man darüber, wie täuschend ähnlich sie dem wirklichen Leben ist. Und zwar nicht, weil AMs Videos die Dramen unserer Nachrichtenfilme und -fotografien so genau imitieren, sondern weil sie das eben gerade nicht tun.

Mick Taussig, November 2006

Jean Rouch
Les Maîtres Fous, 1955

Anmerkungen:

1 Hannah Arendt, ‚Eichmann in Jerusalem: Ein Bericht über die Banalität des Bösen‘, Piper Verlag, München, 1963. Die Sozialwissenschaftlerin Hannah Arendt floh aus Deutschland, nachdem Hitler dort an die Macht gekommen war. Ihr Buch wurde nach ihren Artikeln für The New Yorker über den Eichmann-Prozess veröffentlicht. Während des Prozesses hatte sie beobachtet, dass Eichmann weder ausgeprägte Züge von Antisemitismus zeigte noch irgendeinen psychischen Defekt. Darüber hinaus hatten Psychologen festgestellt, Eichmanns Betragen gegenüber anderen Menschen, vor allem gegenüber seiner Familie und seinen Freunden, sei ‚in hohem Maße wünschenswert‘. Andere Psychologen beobachteten, dass das einzig Anormale an Eichmann sei, dass er sich in Verhalten und Sprache noch ‚normaler‘ zeige als der so genannte Durchschnittsmensch.

2 Walter Benjamin, ‚Kleine Geschichte der Photographie‘ in ‚Das Kunstwerk im Zeitalter seiner technischen Reproduzierbarkeit‘, edition suhrkamp, Frankfurt am Main, 1963 (Erste Auflage), s. 50-51.

3 *Les Maîtres Fous*, (Die verrückten Herren), Film von Jean Rouch, 1954, Länge 35 Minuten. Jean Rouch filmte die jährliche Zeremonie einer religiösen Sekte in Afrika mit Namen Hauka. Wenn sie in Trance waren, bemächtigten sich ihrer verschiedene Geister, die auf stereotype Weise mit kolonialen Autoritäten verbunden waren, u. a. mit dem Generalgouverneur, dem Ingenieur, der Frau des Arztes, dem bösen Major und dem Wachkorporal. Der Film zeigt Menschen mit

rollenden Augen und Schaum vor dem Mund. Sie verspeisen einen geweihten Hund und verbrennen ihre Körper mit Fackeln. Rouchs Film hat auf entscheidende Weise Werner Herzogs Film ‚Herz aus Glas‘ (1975) beeinflusst, in dem Herzog seine Schauspieler hypnotisiert, um dem gesamten eine träumerische Qualität zu verleihen.

4 *Trobriand Cricket: An Ingenious Response to Colonialism*, (Trobriander Kricket: Eine geniale Antwort auf den Kolonialismus), Film von Jerry W. Leach, 1957, Länge 53 Minuten. ‚Trobriander Kricket‘ ist ein berühmter ethnografischer Film. Er zeigt, wie das von methodistischen Missionaren auf den Trobriand Inseln eingeführte Kricketspiel im frühen zwanzigsten Jahrhundert von den Insulanern verändert wurde. Die Trobriander imitieren das traditionell koloniale Spiel nicht in sklavischer Weise, sondern wandeln es um und parodieren es. So wird es Teil einer Anthropologie, die den Europäer erkennen lässt, wie sehr seine eigene Sichtweise von kulturellen Vorurteilen geprägt ist.

Aernout Miks Werke verfügen über einen starken physischen Reiz. Sie fesseln den Betrachter und nehmen ihn in sich auf, so dass er zum Teil ihrer Inszenierung und Handlung wird. Das skulpturale Verhältnis von Wand und Boden und die Interaktion zwischen dem gebauten und gefilmten Raum gehören Grund legend zur Rezeption der Videowerke von Aernout Mik dazu.

<u>Shifting Shifting</u> umfasst vier Werke Miks, die in den letzten achtzehn Monaten entstanden sind: *Vacuum Room* (2005), *Scapegoats* (2006), *Raw Footage* (2006) und *Training Ground* (2006). In überraschender und bizarrer und zugleich ungewöhnlich vertrauter Weise lassen uns diese Filme in ihrem Kern erkennen, wie Macht ausgeübt und immer wieder neu verteilt wird, wie menschliches Verhalten sich wiederholenden Mustern folgt und wie außergewöhnliche Situationen auf beunruhigende Art gewöhnlich sind.

Mit der Ausnahme von *Raw Footage* sind alle diese Werke Fiktionen. Sie haben keinen klaren Anfang und kein eindeutig definiertes Ende. Wie immer, wenn es sich um ein Werk von Mik handelt, gibt es keine klassische Filmerzählung und keine solche Tonspur. Die Handlungen sind hyperrealistisch inszeniert mit einer fast schon absurden Akribie in der Realisierung von Details. Sie berühren in deprimierender Weise viele kollektive ängste unserer Zeit, aber da es sich um Werke von Aernout Mik handelt, tun sie das mit der dem Künstler eigenen leichtfüßigen Eleganz und einem intelligenten Humor.

Raw Footage indes hat Mik aus ausgemustertem, dokumentarischem Filmmaterial hergestellt, das während des Balkankrieges im früheren

Jugoslawien aufgenommen wurde. Es ist inzwischen älter als ein Jahrzehnt und wurde nie gesendet, weil es nicht dramatisch genug war.

Mik benutzt hier zum ersten Mal „gefundenes" Material und enthüllt mit ihm die Banalität des Krieges, die Fernsehsender typischerweise nicht thematisieren. Zugleich erinnert er uns daran, dass gewisse Wahrheiten ebenso seltsam sind wie Fiktionen. Anders als bei seinen sonstigen Werken werden die Bilder hier nicht bis auf den Boden projiziert mit dem Ergebnis, dass der Betrachter sie ähnlich wie beim Fernsehen eher mental als physisch erfährt.

Der Anthropologe Michael Taussig wurde von Mik gebeten, einen Essay für diesen Katalog zu schreiben. Sein profunder Text stellt eindringlich jene Augenblicke des Wiedererkennens heraus, wenn Miks erfundene Welten uns in sehr realistischer Weise menschliches Verhalten und gelebte Erfahrungen vor Augen führen.

Wir danken Michael Taussig sehr für sein Engagement bei diesem Projekt. Und wir danken Irma Boom, die sehr eng mit Aernout Mik an der Gestaltung des wunderschönen Buchs zusammengearbeitet hat, das in harmonischer Weise Werk und Ausstellung begleitet.

Shifting Shifting wurde gemeinschaftlich von vier Kunstinstituten aus vier unterschiedlichen europäischen Ländern organisiert. Uns alle, die wir diesen Instituten vorstehen, eint ein schon lange bestehendes und tief empfundenes Interesse am Werk von Aernout Mik. Die Ausstellungs- und Katalogproduktion wurden von Bruce Haines, Ausstellungsleiter am Camden Arts Centre, sorgfältig koordiniert. Möglich gemacht haben sie die großzügige, alle vier Institute bedenkende, finanzielle Unterstützung

380

der Mondrian Stiftung und der Königlich Niederländischen Botschaft in London. Beide Organisationen können sich ihrer mäzenatischen Haltung rühmen, die sie sowohl gegenüber niederländischen Künstlern einnehmen wie gegenüber den Institutionen, die deren Werke zeigen. Wir danken auch Ulrich Gebauer und Andreas Bunte von der Galerie carlier | gebauer in Berlin, die Aernout Mik als Galeristen vertreten und die bei der Realisierung der Ausstellung eine große Hilfe waren.

Für uns alle war es ein großes Vergnügen, mit Aernout Mik zusammenzuarbeiten. Wir haben von seiner Klugheit, seinem Verstand und seinem Witz profitiert. Vor allem aber waren wir tief beeindruckt, wie engagiert und hart er dafür gearbeitet hat, dass diese vier beeindruckenden Videoinstallationen in London, Edinburg, Bergen und Hannover gezeigt werden können.

Jenni Lomax, Direktorin, Camden Arts Centre, London

zugleich für
Dr. Fiona Bradley, Direktorin, The Fruitmarket Gallery, Edinburgh
Solveig Øvstebø, Direktorin, Bergen Kunsthall
Dr. Stephan Berg, Direktor, Kunstverein Hannover

<u>Videography</u>

2006
Raw Footage; 2 screen video installation;
digital video on hard disc; edition of 4 + 2 a.p.
Scapegoats; video installation;
digital video on hard disc; edition of 4 + 2 a.p.
Training Ground; 2 screen video installation;
digital video on hard disc; edition of 4 + 2 a.p.

2005
Osmosis and Excess; video installation;
digital video on hard disc; edition of 4 + 2 a.p.
Vacuum Room; 6 screen video installation;
digital video on hard disc; edition of 4 + 2 a.p.

2004
Dispersion Room; 2 screen video installation;
digital video on hard disc; edition of 4 + 2 a.p.
Refraction; video installation;
digital video on hard disc; edition of 4 + 2 a.p.

2003
Pulverous; video installation;
digital video on hard disc; edition of 4 + 2 a.p.
Parallel Corner; 4 screen video installation;
digital video on hard disc; edition of 4 + 2 a.p.

2002
Flock; 2 screen video installation;
digital video on dvd; edition of 4 + 1 a.p.
Zone; 4 screen video installation;
digital video in dvd; edition of 4 + 2 a.p.
Park; video installation;
digital video on dvd; edition of 4 + 2 a.p.

2001
Glutinosity; video installation;
digital video on dvd; edition of 4 + 1 a.p.
Reversal Room; 5 screen video installation;
digital video on dvd; edition of 4 + 2 a.p.
Middlemen; video installation;
digital video on dvd; edition of 4 + 1 a.p.

2000
Organic Escalator; video installation;
digital video on dvd; edition of 3 + 1 a.p.
Lumber; 5 screen video installation;
digital video on dvd; edition of 4 + 1 a.p.
Pneumatic Disguise; 2 screen video installation;
digital video on dvd; edition of 4 + 1 a.p.

1999
Piñata; 2 screen video installation;
digital video on dvd; edition of 2 + 1 a.p.
Territorium; 2 screen video installation;
digital video on dvd; edition of 4 + 2 a.p.
Softer Catwalk in Collapsing Rooms; video installation;
digital video on dvd; edition of 2 + 1 a.p.
Swab; video installation;
digital video on dvd; edition of 2 + 1 a.p.

1998
3 laughing and 4 crying; video installation;
digital video on dvd; edition of 2 + 1 a.p.
a small group falling; video installation;
digital video on dvd; edition of 4 + 1 a.p.
Mob; video installation;
digital video on dvd; edition of 4 + 1 a.p.

Float; video installation;
digital video on dvd; edition of 4 + 1 a.p.
Hongkongoria (with Marjoleine Boonstra); video installation;
digital video on dvd; edition of 2 + 1 a.p.
Garage; video installation;
digital video on dvd; edition of 2 + 1 a.p.

1997
Lick; video installation;
digital video on dvd; edition of 2 + 1 a.p.
Kitchen; video installation;
digital video on dvd; edition of 2 + 1 a.p.
Suck; video installation;
digital video on dvd; edition of 2 + 1 a.p.

1996
Fluff; video installation;
s 16 mm film on dvd; edition of 2 + 1 a.p.

1995
Stuffed, Weak and Filthy; film installation;
s 16 mm film; edition of 2 + 1 a.p.

Flock and *Parallel Corner* are courtesy of Galleria Massimo de Carlo, Milan; The Project, LA/NY and carlier | gebauer, Berlin.

Flock is co-produced by Fundació Miró (Barcelona), F.R.A.C. Champagne Ardenne (Reims), Pori Art Museum (Pori, Finland), The Project (New York/Los Angeles), Galleria Massimo de Carlo (Milano) and carlier | gebauer (Berlin).
Pulverous is co-produced with the Stedelijk Museum Amsterdam and Toneelgroep, Amsterdam.
Dispersion Room is co-produced with Haus der Kunst, Munich and was supported by the Netherlands Foundation for Visual Arts, Design and Architecture.
Refraction is co-produced with New Museum, New York, Museum of Contemporary Art, Chicago and UCLA Hammer Museum.
Vacuum Room is co-produced with Centre pour l'image, Geneva and Argos, Brussels.
Osmosis and Excess is co-produced with insite, San Diego.

Various works were supported by the Netherlands Foundation for Visual Arts, Design and Architecture

Aernout Mik

1962
born in Groningen, The Netherlands
lives and works in Amsterdam

Solo exhibitions

2007
LII Venice Biennale, Dutch Pavilion, Italy
Shifting Shifting, Camden Arts Centre, London, UK*
Shifting Shifting, Bergen Kunsthall, Bergen, Norway
Shifting Shifting, The Fruitmarket Gallery, Edinburgh, UK
Shifting Shifting, Kunstverein Hannover, Hannover, Germany

2006
Refraction, UCLA Hammer Museum, Los Angeles, USA
Galleria Massimo de Carlo, Milan, Italy
BAK – Basis voor actuele Kunst, Utrecht, The Netherlands
Galleria Civica di Arte Contemporanea, Trento, Italy

2005
Vacuum Room, MC, Los Angeles, USA
Vacuum Room, carlier | gebauer, Berlin, Germany

Refraction, New Museum of Contemporary Art, New York, USA★
Refraction, Museum of Contemporary Art, Chicago, USA
Vacuum Room, Argos, Brussels, Belgium
Vacuum Room, Centre pour l'image contemporaine, Geneva, Switzerland

2004
Dispersion Room, Ludwig Museum, Cologne, Germany★
Dispersionen, Haus der Kunst, Munich, Germany★
Museo Pasión, Valladolid, Spain
The Project, New York, USA
Herbert F. Johnson Museum of Art, Cornell University, Ithaca, USA

2003
The Cleveland Museum of Art, Cleveland, USA
BildMuseet, Umeå Universität, Umea, Sweden
Porin Taidedmuseo, Pori, Finland
The Project, Los Angeles, USA
Flock, Magasin 3, Stockholm Konsthall, Sweden
Pulverous, carlier | gebauer, Berlin, Germany
Frac Champagne-Ardenne, Reims, France
CaixaForum, Barcelona, Spain★
Les Abbatoirs, Toulouse, France
In Two Minds, co-production with Toneelgroep Amsterdam,
Stedelijk Museum Amsterdam, The Netherlands

2002
Reversal Room, Stedelijk Museum Bureau Amsterdam, The Netherlands
AM in the LAM, The Living Art Museum, Reykjavik, Iceland
Fundació Miro, Barcelona, Spain
CAC, Vilnius, Lithuania
Galleria Massimo di Carlo, Milano, Italy

2001
Domaine de Kerguéhennec, Bignan, France
Reversal Room, The Powerplant, Toronto, Canada★
Middlemen, carlier | gebauer, Berlin, Germany

2000
Primal Gestures, *Minor Roles*, Van Abbe Museum, Eindhoven,
The Netherlands★
Simulantengang, Kasseler Kunstverein, Kassel, Germany
Tender Habitat, Jean Paul Slusser Gallery, The University of Michigan,
Ann Arbor, USA
3 Crowds, ICA, London, UK★

1999
Small Disasters, Galerie Fons Welters, Amsterdam, The Netherlands
Hanging Around, Projektraum Museum Ludwig, Köln, Germany★
Softer Catwalk in Collapsing Rooms, Galerie Gebauer, Berlin, Germany

1998
Galerie Index, Stockholm, Sweden

1997
XLVII Venice Biennale, Dutch Pavilion (with Willem Oorebeek), Italy⋆

1995
Mommy I am sorry (with Adam Kalkin), De Vleeshal, Middelburg,
The Netherlands⋆
Wie die Räume gefüllt werden müssen, Kunstverein Hannover, Germany⋆
Stuffed, Weak and Filthy, Deweer Art Gallery, Otegem, Belgium

⋆ indicates publication of a catalogue

Acknowledgements

Aernout Mik and Camden Arts Centre would like to thank the following individuals and organisations for their invaluable assistance in the organisation of the exhibition, publication and production of work:

Jenni Lomax, Director; Bruce Haines, Exhibition Organiser &
Richard Gough, Gallery Manager, Camden Arts Centre, London
Dr. Fiona Bradley, Director, The Fruitmarket Gallery, Edinburgh
Solveig Øvstebø, Director, Bergen Kunsthall, Norway
Prof. Dr. Stephan Berg, Director, Kunstverein Hannover

Marie-Blanche Carlier, Ulrich Gebauer,
Andreas Bunte, carlier | gebauer, Berlin
Christian Haye, The Project, New York
Jozef Hey, Beamsystems, Amsterdam
Maria Hlavajova, BAK, Utrecht
Matthew Keene, ITN, London
Angela Lautenbach, Hannover
Jorma Saarikko, Pro Av, Finland
Mick Taussig, New York
Irma Boom, Sonja Haller, Amsterdam

Credits

Raw Footage: Research: Danila Cahen; Mixage/Sound engineering: Hugo Dijkstal; Online: Joke Treffers; Images from found documentary material: Reuters & ITN (ITN Source). Courtesy *Raw Footage* galerie carlier | gebauer, Berlin.

Scapegoats: Production: Dirk Tolman, Jelier & Schaaf; Director of Photography: Benito Strangio; Steady-cam: Jo Vermaercke; Co-direction: Marjoleine Boonstra; Art-direction: Elsje de Bruijn; Casting: Hans Kemna & Kemna Casting; Costumes: Sylvia Huijerman; Camera equipment: Cam-a-lot; Production manager: Wikke van der Burg; Make-up: Niels Wahlers; Weapon handlers and fight instructors: Rik and Harry Wiessenhaan; Special Effects: Rob's Prop Shop; Grip: Enterprise; Photography on set: Florian Braun; Post production: Loods lux & lumen and Beamsystems. Courtesy *Scapegoats* galerie carlier | gebauer, Berlin.

Raw Footage & *Scapegoats* are produced by the artist and BAK realised in partnership with Treaty of Utrecht. Additional support generously provided by The Netherlands Foundation for Visual Arts, Design and Architecture; Mondriaan Foundation; Galleria Civica di Arte Contemporanea, Trento; ThuisKopie Fonds and Fentener van Vlissingen Fonds.

Training Ground is produced by the artist and realised courtesy carlier | gebauer and The Project, New York. Collection: Dennis and Debra Scholl, Miami, USA. Production: Dirk Tolman, Jelier & Schaaf, Anca Munteanu; Steady-cam: Benito Strangio, Jo Vermaercke; Co-direction: Marjoleine Boonstra; Art Direction: Elsje de Bruijn; Costumes: Elisabetta Pian; Fight instructor: Rik Wiessenhaan; Casting: Anca Munteanu; Art department: Josche Allwardt; Photography on set: Florian Braun.

Vacuum Room is co-produced with Argos, Brussels and Centre pour l'Image Contemporaine, Geneva. Production: Dirk Tolman, Jelier & Schaaf; Co-direction: Marjoleine Boonstra; Art Direction: Elsje de Bruijn; Costumes: Sylvia Huijerman; Casting: Hans Kemna & Kemna Casting; Camera techniek: beamsystems.

Published on the occasion of the exhibition Aernout Mik: 'Shifting Shifting' organised by Camden Arts Centre with The Fruitmarket Gallery, Edinburgh; Bergen Kunsthall and Kunstverein Hannover.

<u>Exhibition schedule</u>

Camden Arts Centre, London
16 February – 15 April 2007

Arkwright Road, London NW3 6DG, England
Tel +44 (0)20 7472.55.00; Fax +44 (0)20 7472.55.01
www.camdenartscentre.org

The Fruitmarket Gallery, Edinburgh
19 May – 15 July 2007

45 Market St, Edinburgh EH1 3PA, Scotland
Tel +44 (0)131 225.23.83; Fax +44 (0)131 220.31.30
www.fruitmarket.co.uk

Bergen Kunsthall
7 September – 28 October 2007

Rasmus Meyers Allé 5, 5015 Bergen, Norway
Tel +47 55 55.93.10; Fax +47 55 55.93.19
www.kunsthall.no

Kunstverein Hannover
8. December 2007 – 3.February 2008

Sophienstrasse 2, 30159 Hannover, Germany
Tel +49 (0)5 11 32.45.94; Fax +49 (0)511 363.22.47
www.kunstverein-hannover.de

Published by Camden Arts Centre, London, 2007

ISBN 978 1 900470 63 6
Printed in an edition of 1200

Edited by Bruce Haines
Text by Michael Taussig
Designed by Irma Boom Office, Amsterdam
(Irma Boom, Sonja Haller)
Translation by Michael Stoeber
Printed by Rosbeek, Nuth

Camden Arts Centre
Registered charity 1065829/0
Registered company 2947191
Registered office: Arkwright Road, London, NW3 6DG
Vat reg. no 586 9041 03

Distributed by

Art Data International

12 Bell Industrial Estate, 50 Cunnington Street, London W4 5HB, UK
Tel +44 (0) 208 747.10.61; Fax +44 (0) 208 742.23.19

Cornerhouse Publications

70 Oxford Street, Manchester M1 5NH, UK
Tel +44 (0)161 200.15.03; Fax +44 (0)161 200.15.04
www.cornerhouse.org/publications

The exhibition *Shifting Shifting* is supported by the Mondriaan Foundation and in London by the Royal Netherlands Embassy. Aernout Mik has received support from the Netherlands Foundation for Visual Arts, Design and Architecture.

Camden Arts Centre is supported by Arts Council England and London Borough of Camden

The Fruitmarket Gallery is supported by Scottish Arts Council

Bergen Kunsthall receives support from Bergen Kommune and Norsk Kulturråd

KUNSTHALL
NO 5   LANDMARK

The exhibition at Kunstverein Hannover has received support from Eon Energy and Eon:Is and the cultural department of the Landeshauptstadt Hannover